DATE DUE

JUN. 27 1983	JA 22 '87	JY 12 '90
JUN. 30 1983	JY 20 '87	NOV 30
AUG. 26 1983	DE 9 '87	JAN 31
MAR. 2 1984	MR 12 '88	AG 02
JUN. 15 1984	JE 30 '88	JUN 1 1
AUG 07 1984	JY 27 '88	JU 16
SEP. 28 1984	MR 3 '89	JL 16
DEC. 13 1984	14 '89 Y 09 '08	NOV 20
OC 12 '85	NO 24	AG 18 '00
SE 3 '86	JA 23 90	JY 09 0
	JE 26 '90	
		JE 23 '08

THE
GREEN BAY PACKERS

THE GREEN BAY PACKERS

JULIAN MAY

**C CREATIVE EDUCATION, INC.
MANKATO, MINNESOTA 56001**

PHOTOGRAPHIC CREDITS:

John Biever: 11, 14, 26; Vernon J. Biever: 2-3, 10, 12, 13, 15, 16, 17, 18, 19, 24, 25, 27, 29, 30, 32, 33, 36, 37, 41, 42, 43, 45, 46, 47; Clarence Bredell: 6; Rich Clarkson: 21; Hank Lefebvre: 8; Green Bay Packers: 9; United Press International: 20, 22, 23, 34, 38, 40; Wide World: 28.

Library of Congress Number: 80-68930   ISBN: 0-87191-727-0

Published by Creative Education, Inc., Mankato, Minnesota 56001

THE
GREEN BAY PACKERS

Earl "Curly" Lambeau, Packer coach for 30 years, played with the team until 1929. Almost single-handedly he built the Packers into a first-rate football force. In the early days, when the team threatened to fold because it needed money, citizens of Green Bay came to its rescue. Urged on by Lambeau, members of the community bought shares in the Packers. Today the team is still owned by a nonprofit community corporation. Home games are played in Lambeau Field and Milwaukee County Stadium.

BIRTH OF A LEGEND

Back in 1919, when the Green Bay Packers were born, there was no NFL. A few pro football teams existed — like the Canton Bulldogs, the Columbus Panhandles, the Detroit Heralds, and the Massillon Tigers. They are all gone now but the Green Bay Packers live on.

The Packers were founded by a young man named Earl (Curly) Lambeau. He worked for a meat-packing company in the small city of Green Bay, Wisconsin. When Lambeau told his boss about wanting to start a team, the company contributed $500. Curly became the manager, coach, and star running back. He named the team the ''Packers'' in honor of the company that helped get it started.

The Packers won ten straight games in 1919. But they lost the area championship to the Beloit Fairies! In 1921, the Packers joined the American Professional Football Association. Later, this group became the NFL.

Under Curly Lambeau the Packers became the first team to use the passing game. They were NFL champs in 1929, 1930, and 1931. Some of the ''iron men'' who played on those early Packer teams were later honored in the Hall of Fame — men such as Johnny McNally, Cal Hubbard, and Mike Michalske. In many games, 12 or 13 players would be on the field for almost the entire 60 minutes, playing both offense and defense.

Old-time Packer superstars included "Johnny Blood" McNally, a charter member of football's Hall of Fame. He was a brilliant halfback whose fast thinking and speed pulled many a Packer victory out of the fire. Playing for the sheer love of it, his crazy stunts on and off the field made him a legend. He once said that his aim was "to be as amusing and spectacular as possible."

Packer guard August "Mike" Michalske, another Hall-of-Famer, played for Green Bay from 1929 until 1937. He was elected to the roster of football immortals in 1964.

Cal Hubbard began his career with the New York Giants. Another charter member of the Hall of Fame, he played tackle and end for the Packers from 1929 until 1935. Along with McNally and Michalske, he was selected for the first All-Pro Team in 1931.

Don Hutson joined the Packers in 1935. In his first game, he caught a 50-yard pass and ran 33 yards for a touchdown against the Chicago Bears. He and quarterback Don Isbell became an unbeatable passing combination. In 118 games played, he caught 489 passes, gained 8,010 yards, and scored 100 touchdown passes. He was among the first group elected to football's Hall of Fame.

Stars such as fullback Clarke Hinkle and quarterback Arnie Herber shone for the Pack during the early 1930's. But the team did not win another championship until the coming of Don Hutson.

He was a slender, speedy end known as the "Arkansas Antelope," one of the greatest pass receivers of all time. During his ten years with the Packers, the team won three more NFL titles (1936, 1939, 1944). When Hutson finally retired in 1945, he took Green Bay's heart along with him.

9

The team was in the dumps for 14 terrible years as four different coaches tried to find a formula for success. Curly Lambeau retired in 1949. Gene Ronzani, Lisle Blackbourn, and Ray (Scooter) McLean all had their chance and failed. Players felt that getting sent to Green Bay was like being exiled to Siberia. The 1958 Packer record was the worst ever — 1-10-1.

The team had talented players. But it lacked discipline. Green Bay management looked around for a tough coach who could make the men shape up.

The person they hired was a fiery assistant for the New York Giants, Vince Lombardi.

Lombardi told the players, "I have never been on a losing team and I don't intend to start now. I want total dedication . . . total dedication to *winning*."

"Your first task is to make yourselves physically fit. Your second task is to sharpen your mental alertness. And your third task is to develop the winning habit. Winning isn't everything — it's the *only* thing. And I intend to win."

Lombardi was a hard taskmaster. He never let up. The men groaned and worked harder than they ever had before. And on September 27, 1959, they won their season opener against their old rivals, the Chicago Bears. A new era had begun.

At first, tough Vince Lombardi thought Bart Starr (15) was too "nice and quiet" to be a quarterback.

The Packer quarterback, Lamar McHan, was hurt after several games. Lombardi started the backup, a young man named Bart Starr.

In his first starting game, Starr faced the great Johnny Unitas of Baltimore. The Colts won that game, but it was a 28-24 squeaker. For the rest of the season, Coach Lombardi stuck with Starr.

The team won their last four games in a row and Starr was a standout! The Packers finished 7-5, their first winning season since 1947.

Vince Lombardi was selected Coach of the Year.

The 1961 NFL title game was the first ever played in Green Bay. Earlier Packer title games were played in warmer cities. Here the happy fans swarm over the goalposts after the game.

START OF THE GOLDEN AGE

In 1960, the Packers were 8-4, champions of the Western Division. They faced Philadelphia in the NFL title game as underdogs. Even though Green Bay battled the 10-2 Eagles to the very end, they lost the championship, 17-13.

Lombardi worked the team harder than ever in 1961. They finished 11-3. The title game, against New York, was played in an icy wind. The Giants never did manage to thaw out and Green Bay triumphed, 37-0, while delighted fans shrieked, "Titletown USA!"

For the first time since 1944, the Green Bay Packers were football champions of the world.

13

The Packers were 13-1-0 in 1962. Bart Starr had passed for 2,438 yards. Jim Taylor rushed 1,474 yards and got 19 touchdowns. Willie Wood was the number one interceptor.

Once again the NFL championship was fought between Green Bay and the New York Giants. With the score 10-7 in the third quarter, both defenses stiffened. Green Bay's Jerry Kramer scored one field goal — then another with less than two minutes left. The Packers won, 16-7, and were world champions once again.

Mountainous linebacker Ray Nitschke looms over a hapless foe who appears to have collapsed from sheer fright.

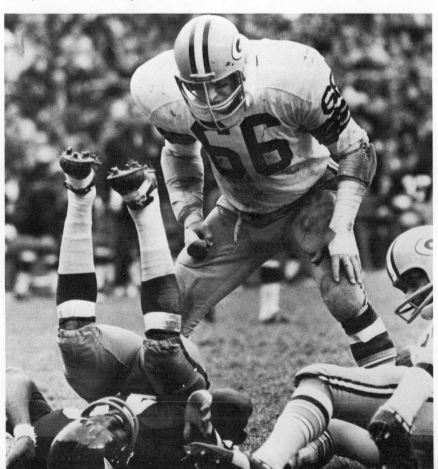

Dejected Bart Starr, Forrest Gregg, and Dan Grimm reflect the feelings of the during a 1964 game against the Baltimore Colts. The Packers lost.

Vince Lombardi longed to repeat Curly Lambeau's Triple Crown title series. But 1963 began very badly. Star fullback Paul Hornung was suspended for betting on games.

Then the entire Green Bay team suffered an unusual humiliation: They lost the College All-Star game, 20-17!

Burning mad, Lombardi pounded his overconfident warriors back into top shape. The Packer record that year was excellent 11-2-1. But the Chicago Bears finished 11-1-2, wrapping up the Western Conference title by half a game.

The next year was worse. Hornung was back, but

Don Chandler kicks the winning field goal in the 1965 title game making the Packers Western Conference champs.

rusty. His failures in conversions and field-goal attempts cost the Pack two important games.

The Packers came in second again, with a record of 8-5-1.

"You're still a first-place team," Lombardi told his dejected troops. "You just quit paying the price. *This* season, you're going to pay . . ."

Lombardi hired ace punter Don Chandler from the Giants. The Packers then came to the end of the 1965 season neck and neck with the Colts.

In the deciding game, Starr was injured and sub Zeke Bratkowski took over. He led the team to a 10-10 tie and into sudden death. Bratkowski moved the Pack to the

16

Colt 25. There Chandler kicked the winning field goal, giving Green Bay the Western Conference title.

The 1965 NFL title game was played in Green Bay on a snowy, foggy day. The Packers faced the Cleveland Browns.

At the half, the score was 13-12 with the Pack on top. Paul Hornung racked up a Packer touchdown in the third period, while the Browns were held scoreless. A 29-yard field goal by Chandler in the last quarter wrapped up the NFL title for Green Bay, 23-12.

THE FIRST SUPER BOWL

Since 1960, there had been two football leagues in the United States. The new American Football League rival-

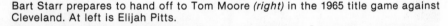

Bart Starr prepares to hand off to Tom Moore (right) in the 1965 title game against Cleveland. At left is Elijah Pitts.

Packer end Boyd Dowler sails through the air for a touchdown during the 1966 NFL title game between Green Bay and Dallas. Green Bay won, 34-27.

18

Lombardi and ace kicker Don Chandler (34).

ed the older NFL. At first, AFL teams were much weaker than those of the NFL. But as years went by, the AFL became stronger. It began to lure away good players from the NFL. Even worse, it outbid the NFL in the draft of college stars.

The two leagues finally agreed to make peace in 1966. They would share a common draft. And the top teams of the two leagues would meet at the end of the season in a "Super Bowl" contest to decide the world championship.

The Packers wanted that Super Bowl trophy. All through the 1966 season they battled to prove they were the best. But it was a very close race. They won the NFL title in a playoff against the Dallas Cowboys by a score of only 34-27.

Then they prepared to meet the AFL Kansas City Chiefs in the Super Bowl.

Super Bowl I started with a kickoff by the Chiefs' Duck Smith. The ball sailed to the Packer 5-yard line,

19

where Herb Adderley caught it and returned it to the 25.

Bart Starr took over. He called a series of cautious running plays, testing the Kansas City defense. It consisted of wild blitzes. Packer flanker Boyd Dowler was injured on the sixth play. Lombardi sent in 12-year veteran Max McGee, who had planned to retire after the Super Bowl.

The crowd, rooting for underdog Kansas City, howled happily as Starr was red-dogged on pass attempts. Forced to punt, the Packers seemed to be a slow, drab team.

Bart Starr manages to keep a grip on the ball as he is smothered by the Chiefs' Buck Buchanan (86) and Ed Holub (55). Packer Forrest Gregg (75) goes down in front of Starr while Jerry Mays of Kansas City (75) comes in.

Max McGee, snaring a pass on the Kansas City 19, sprints for a touchdown.

The Chiefs played their own brand of fancy offense and managed a first down. But then the Packer defense stood firm and the Chiefs had to punt.

Green Bay's second series of offensive plays led to the Kansas City 37. There Starr called for a pass to old Max McGee. Chief cornerback Willie Mitchell tried to intercept in vain. The ball struck McGee's hand and bounced upward. With Mitchell closing in, McGee caught the ball with one hand *behind his back*. Then he ran 19 yards for a Packer touchdown.

The Chiefs didn't seem impressed. In the second quarter they snowed the Packer defense with play-action. Curt McClinton scored a touchdown for Kansas City. With the conversion, the score stood at 7-7.

Bart Starr, his aerial game shot down by Chief blitzers, called for a good old-fashioned power sweep. He handed off to Jim Taylor. Jerry Kramer and Fuzzy Thurston shepherded the fullback across the goal-line for a second Green Bay touchdown. Don Chandler kicked the extra point.

Chief quarterback Len Dawson began a march that carried his team to the Green Bay 31. There they settled for a field goal as the half ended with the score at 14-10.

Bart Starr (15) tries for a pass as Kansas City defenders close in on him.

NFL Commissioner Alvin "Pete" Rozell *(left)* presents the Super Bowl trophy to Vince Lombardi. The trophy was later named after the famous Green Bay coach.

It seemed as though the football upset of the century was in the making.

Lombardi sailed into his team in the locker room. "Are you the world champion Green Bay Packers or aren't you?" he yelled furiously. "Get out on that field and answer me!"

The second half saw the Pack up to its old standard. The Packer defense surprised Dawson with a blitz. His wobbly pass was retrieved by Packer safety Willie Wood, who ran the ball to the Kansas City 5-yard line. Elijah Pitts crashed into the end zone for a touchdown.

From then on, it was a rout. The Chiefs could not get past the Packer 44-yard line. Green Bay was in control. Max McGee accounted for another touchdown and Elijah Pitts added a fifth for good measure.

The final score was Green Bay 35, Kansas City 10.

And there was no doubt in anybody's mind which team was champion of the world.

The Super Bowl was really only a sideshow to Vince Lombardi. His real challenge was the triple crown, three NFL titles in a row. In 1967, Green Bay didn't seem to have a prayer. Jim Taylor and Paul Hornung were gone to other teams. Bart Starr was injured in exhibition games. Early in the season, so many other Packers were hurt that assistant coach Phil Bengtson referred to the team as the "walking wounded."

Despite this, they wrapped up the Central Division with a record of 9-4-1. In the semifinals, Green Bay beat Los Angeles, 28-7.

Frigid temperatures could not keep Green Bay fans away from the 1967 NFL title game, played on December 31.

For the NFL title, the Packers met the Dallas Cowboys again. The game they played was one of the most amazing in football history. Later, fans called it the "Ice Bowl." It was played with the temperature at 13 below zero.

Green Bay led at the start of the fourth quarter, 14-10. But then Dallas rallied and slid ahead, 17-14. And the Pack just couldn't seem to snap back. The last period ticked away as a chill colder than the arctic wind settled over the Green Bay fans. They awaited icy doom.

Then, with four minuites to go, the Packers mounted a drive from their own 31-yard line. They struggled to the Dallas 45, to the 42. With a minute and half left, they had reached the 30. Then rookie back Chuck Mer-

Bart Starr's quarterback sneak yields the winning touchdown of the exciting "Ice Bowl" game. Other Packers in view are Chuck Mercein (30), Marv Fleming (81), and Jerry Kramer (64).

cein managed to go out of bounds on the 11 and stop the clock.

Now Bart Starr took advantage of every opening. The Pack hammered in to the one-yard line. With only 13 seconds left, Starr plunged into the end zone on a quarterback sneak.

The Packers won, 21-17. The NFL title and triple crown had come to roost in Green Bay.

THE SECOND SUPER BOWL

They called the Oakland Raiders' defense the "Angry Eleven." Throughout the 1967 season, they had proved that they were the best in the AFL. Also tops was the Raiders' cool young quarterback, Daryle Lamonica. His backup man was veteran George Blanda, whose "Golden Toe" had kicked 20 field goals that season

Could the Packers beat this strong, young team? Lombardi called the men together after their last Super Bowl practice session. He said, "We all know we can win our second Super Bowl Trophy Sunday . . . I want to tell you how very proud I am of all of you. It's been a long

Howie Williams (29), Oakland defensive back, breaks up a Bart Starr pass to Max McGee (85) during Super Bowl II.

season, and Sunday may be the last time we are all together. Let's make it a game we can be proud of.''

The players all looked at the ground. Some of them felt tears come to their eyes. They knew what the coach meant. He was planning to retire. This was the last time he would lead the team he had single-handedly turned into champions.

Super Bowl II was played in Miami. Under the warm Florida sun, the Packers played the last game for Vince.

Don Chandler scored with field goals in the first and second quarters. Then Boyd Dowler rang the bell again for the Pack by scoring on a 62-yard pass from Bart Starr. With Chandler's extra point, the score stood at 13-0.

Oakland then began a march that ended with Daryle Lamonica passing to Bill Miller for 23 yards and a touchdown. There was only a minute left in the first half when the Packers punted. Rodger Bird of the Raiders dropped the ball, allowing Green Bay to recover on the 45-yard line.

With only seconds remaining, Don Chandler kicked a third field goal.

The third quarter saw the last great play of Max McGee. (He had decided to play one final season for Green Bay.) Bart Starr called a "36 pass," a play McGee knew very well. First Starr faked a handoff to fullback Ben Wilson. Then, with the Raider defense braced for a run, Starr fired a short pass to McGee, who had broken around the Raider cornerback. McGee ran 35 yards to the Oakland 23, setting up a touchdown a few plays later.

Bart Starr and Coach Phil Bengtson discuss strategy during a 1969 game.

Oakland could not recover the advantage. The game ended with a score of 33-14 — the Green Bay Packers' second Super Bowl victory in a row.

Jerry Kramer and Forrest Gregg hoisted Vince Lombardi to their shoulders as the cheers rang out.

"This," said Coach Lombardi, "is the best way to leave a football field."

A HARD ACT TO FOLLOW

During 1968, Vince Lombardi served as General Manager of the Packers. But he was restless in the front office and decided to go back to coaching. He had hand-picked Phil Bengtson as his successor at Green Bay, so there was no thought of his taking over the Packers again.

Lombardi went to the Washington Redskins. In one year, he turned them from losers to winners. Then the great coach died of cancer in 1970. The entire football world mourned. But in no city was the sorrow as great as in Green Bay.

Phil Bengtson simply could not fill Vince Lombardi's shoes. He was a friendly man and the team like him. But he was not the hard taskmaster that Lombardi had been — and the Green Bay team needed a firm hand at the helm. The Pack lost its division title to Baltimore in 1968 when it finished with a 6-7-1 record. The following year, the team was 8-6, third in the Central Division.

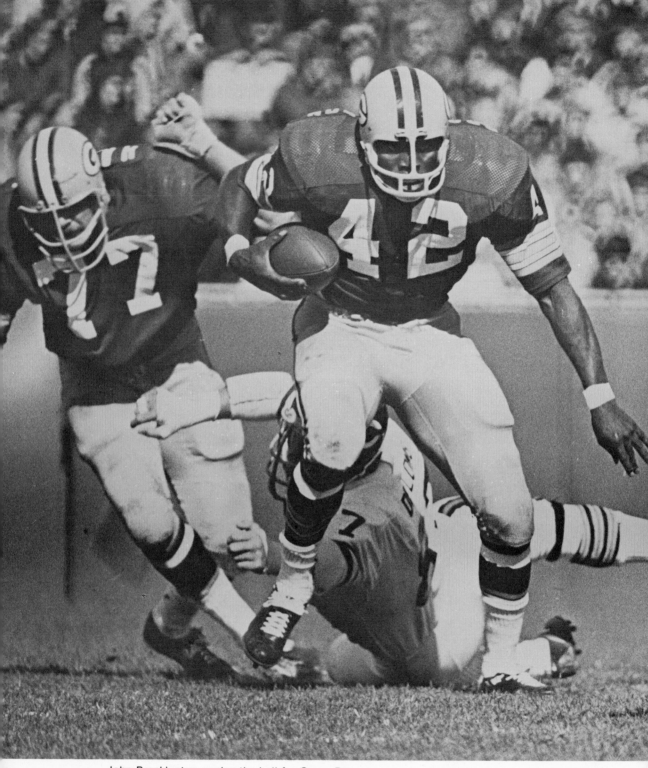

John Brockington carries the ball for Green Bay.

Green Bay Coach Dan Devine *(right)* is joined on the sidelines by Coach Paul Brown, who pioneered "scientific" football.

One of the problems was Bart Starr. He had injured his passing arm, but he continued to play in pain because he "didn't want to let Coach Bengtson down."

Starr's arm got worse and worse. The Packers were 6-8 in 1970, in the division cellar. Bengtson resigned after the losing season. Starr did special exercises that were supposed to help his arm. But he was hurt again in 1971 and missed the entire pre-season as well as ten regular games.

Bart came back towards the end of the season to try to help his sagging team. Under new coach Dan Devine, a college whiz, the Pack finished 4-8-2. But many of their losses had been narrow ones.

The next year, even though Bart Starr had to retire, Green Bay took the Central Division title with a 10-4 record.

33

Packer defenders Mike McCoy (76) and Alden Roche (87) hold back Minnesota's Bill Brown during a 1972 contest. Green Bay won, 23-7.

They lost the playoff to Washington, 16-3. But fans crowed: "The Pack is back!"

One of the new stars was a rusher named John Brockington. He had been Rookie of the Year in 1971. In that year and in 1972 he had gained more than 1,000 yards — an NFL record-breaker.

Another player who made the 1972 season sparkle was kicker Chester Marcol. In his first year he booted 33 field goals, tops in the NFL, winning Rookie of the Year honors. He would become one of the leading kickers in the league during years to come.

Despite Brockington and Marcol and other fine players the Packers were only 5-7-2 in 1973. Key players suffered injuries — and none of the three young quarterbacks that Coach Devine started was able to do a competent job.

The recession continued in 1974. Coach Devine traded away many critical draft choices in order to obtain an experienced quarterback. John Hadl came to Green Bay from Los Angeles. In 1973 he had been the NFC's Most Valuable Player. But he was already 34 years old. His completion percentage for the Packers in 1974 was a disappointing 47.5.

On the other hand, Chester Marcol was league-leading scorer with 94 points — 25 field goals and 19 PAT's. His performance could not make up for other team lacks. Green Bay wound up with a dismal 6-8 record in 1974. Coach Devine resigned — the second

Rabid Green Bay fans whoop it up for their team.

man to fail in trying to follow Vince Lombardi's triumph.

Who can measure up to a legend? Who even wants to try it?

That was the problem facing management in Green Bay. The fans were getting very impatient. Bumper-stickers read: IT'S TIME THE PACK CAME BACK!

But getting a coach who could accomplish the miracle was not going to be easy. There was much rebuilding to be done — and many draft choices had been squandered on Hadl, who was on his way down and out. In 1975, the coach who stepped in would have to tough-out some hard years. He would have to be an outstanding and brave man.

36

Bart Starr addresses reporters after being named Packer coach.

Lynn Dickey passes for a touchdown during the 1976 pre-season opener against Cincinnati. Providing coverage is fullback Barty Smith (33).

Green Bay found the man. His name was Bart Starr.

When he took over as skipper, he said, "We will need the prayers and patience of Packer fans everywhere. We will earn everythng else."

THE PACK COMES BACK

Bart Starr's coaching experience was limited to a single season in 1972, when he had helped guide quarterbacks under Devine. He had been one of the greatest field generals in NFL history, but he was going to learn the coaching trade mostly through on-the-job training!

It would be a tough haul. But fans who had been merciless with luckless Devine would turn into pussycats when Bart Starr, Living Legend No. 2, asked them to wait while he rebuilt the team.

Bart and the fans had to settle for a 4-10 record in 1975. Kicker Marcol was out for the entire season with an injury. Quarterback Hadl, on a downhill slide, suffered 21 interceptions. The once-great rusher, Brockington, gained only 434 yards and seemed to be fading fast but the Pack won three of the last five games that year. And Steve Odom blossomed as an outstanding kickoff return artist, logging 1,034 yards.

In 1976, Starr traded Hadl to Houston for young quarterback Lynn Dickey. In the draft, he acquired Mark Koncar, who put in an All-Rookie honor performance. The Packers wound up with a 5-9 record.

Slowly, the Pack was coming back.

The 1977 season began with a victory over New Orleans. After that, four near misses followed, dampening the spirits of the young Packers.

After a hollow win over the pathetic Tampa Bay team, the Pack bowed in two more contests. In the latter game, against the Rams, fans booed Lynn Dickey until his leg was broken in the final play.

Bart Starr put in rookie quarterback David Whitehurst the following week. He showed great promise in his debut, playing before national TV. In spite of three interceptions and six sacks, the game against the Redskins was close — Washington 10, Green Bay 9.

Whitehurst settled in to a 2-2 record on the last four games — and the losses were narrow.

Lynn Dickey is placed in an ambulance after breaking his leg. The injury finished him for the 1977 season.

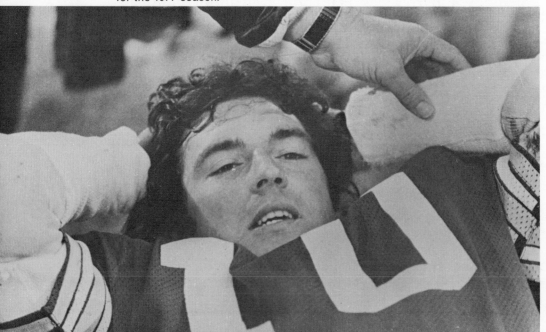

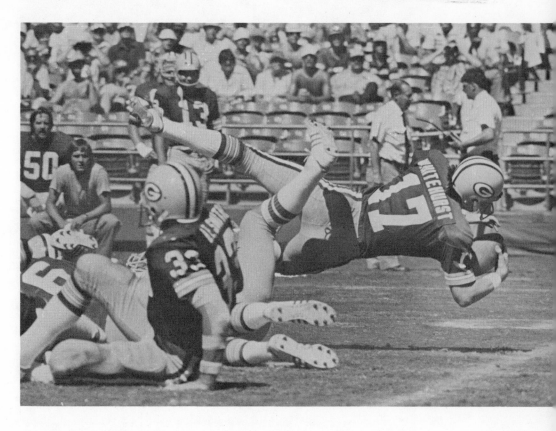

David Whitehurst bites the dust during a 1978 game.

Dickey's leg was still weak in 1978, and so Whitehurst was installed as permanent starter. Bart Starr had great hopes for the team that season. And so did the Green Bay fans. The year 1978 marked the Packers' 60th year as a pro football club. No other NFL team had stayed so long in the city of its birth. In fact, no other had endured so long.

In Game 1, the Pack whipped Detroit, 13-7. The next contest saw Whitehurst throw four touchdown passes for a 27-17 victory over New Orleans.

It was a great beginning.

Willie Buchanon holds the ball high as he gallops along the sidelines during the game against San Diego, played on September 24, 1978. Johnnie Gray (24) rides shotgun, fending off Charger Lydell Mitchell (26).

After four games the Pack was 3 and 1.

"The Pack is back! It's *really* back!" howled the fans. In the next game they saw the Green Bay team score more points in one game than they had in the past three years as they defeated the Lions, 35-14.

Yes, they were getting it all together at last. White-hurst was doing splendidly as field general. Chester Marcol was healthy and kicking up a storm. And sophomore rusher Terdell Middleton had put long-awaited zip in the ground game. The defense was looking fine —

42

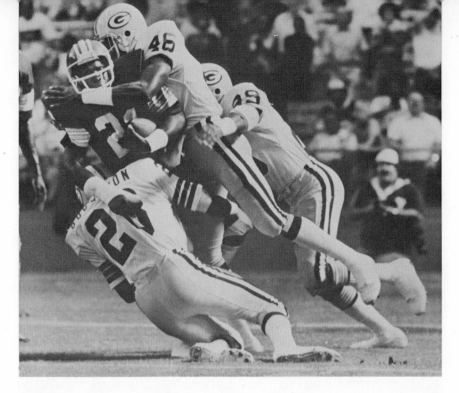

The famous SWAT secondary does its thing. Featured are Willie Buchanon (28), Steve Luke (46), Mike McCoy (29), and Johnnie Gray (24).

especially the secondary of Buchanon, Mike C. McCoy, Johnnie Gray, and Steve Luke — who called themselves SWAT.

The Packers beat Chicago and they beat Seattle, making them 6-1.

The Seattle coach said of the Packers: ''They may not have the great names today — but their day is coming.''

The Pack was leading the Central Division when they met the Minnesota Vikings, now a club of aging superstars. Minnesota won, 21-7.

The showdown came when they met Minnesota again in Game 13. According to the complex rules of the new 16-game season, Green Bay had to beat the Vikings or else see its playoff slot endangered.

And for the first 58 minutes of the ball game, it looked like they were going to do it.

The third period was scoreless. In the final quarter, the Packers scored with a second field goal and it was 10-3 with two minutes remaining.

Frank Tarkenton of the Vikings sent pass after pass for short yardage. Minnesota battled the Green Bay defense — especially the ferocious defensive ends Ezra Johnson and Mike Butler. Tarkenton reached the Packer 5-yard line with just 14 seconds remaining.

Green Bay's Mike McCoy was hovering around Viking receiver Amad Rashad. But Tarkenton chanced a pass into the end zone — and Rashad narrowly made the grab for the tying touchdown.

The game went into overtime — but neither team could score, and so it ended 10-10. But under the rules, Minnesota now had a leading edge over the Packers in their division.

"We still control our own fate," said Bart Starr. But all playoff hopes now hung on the last game.

The Packers played the Rams in Los Angeles on a gloomy, rainy day. Despite two scoring runs by Terdell Middleton, they were defeated, 31-14, and eliminated from the playoffs.

But it had been an 8-7-1 winning season, their first since 1972.

The 1979 season started with a 3-6 loss to the Chicago Bears. It was an omen of things to come.

44

Almost immediately the Packers were plagued by injuries. Before the season was over the Pack had a team record for hurt players and a season score-card that read 5 and 11.

Bart Starr's coaching future seemed to be in doubt. Since the Coach took over in 1975, there had been many inconsistencies in the Packers form. Injury plagued, they had only occassional success, season after season. Up one year, down the next, the Packers had chalked up just one winning year since 1972.

The Green Bay ownership and the team kept faith with Bart Starr. In 1980 there was a slight improvement. No more wins, but the Pack registered one less loss. The season ended 5-10-1.

Chester Marcol catches his breath after booting a field goal in the crucial 1978 game against the Vikings. Bob Douglass (19) held the ball.

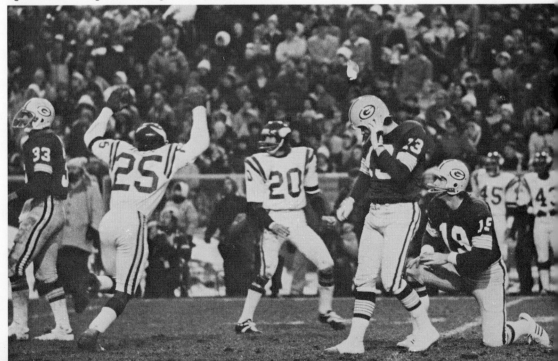

Again there were rumblings about the Coach, and again the decision was to stand by their man. In 1981, it seemed to begin to pay off.

In an early season trade, Coach Bart Starr brought All-Pro receiver John Jefferson to Green Bay from San Diego. Critics said he was buying somebody else's trouble and when the season started out slow, Starr took the heat.

Then, in the second half, things began to come together. Jefferson played like the All-Pro the coach knew him to be and James Lofton reminded the Michigan crowd of his own All-Pro status. Lynn Dickey ranged freely behind an immoveable offensive line and completed 204 passes for the fourth highest rating in the NFC.

The Packers won six of their last eight games. The team began to believe they could be winners, and '82 seemed a season to look forward to.

"I think we accomplished a lot this season," the Coach said of 1981, and Packer fans everywhere had to agree.

As snowflakes drift down, Bart Starr and assistant Zeke Bratkowski study the situation.

GREEEN BAY PACKERS

Founded in 1919, the Packers joined the American Professional Football Association (later the NFL) in 1921. Of all those long-ago teams, only the Packers retain their original name and original home city.

The 1979 season marked the Packer's 60th year in football.

RECORD

Year	Won	Lost	Tied	Pct.
1921	6	2	2	.750
1922	4	3	3	.571
1923	7	2	1	.778
1924	8	4	0	.667
1925	8	5	0	.615
1926	7	3	3	.700
1927	7	2	1	.778
1928	6	4	3	.600
1929	12	0	1	.961
1930	10	3	1	.769
1931	12	2	0	.857
1932	10	3	1	.769
1933	5	7	1	.417
1934	7	6	0	.538
1935	8	4	0	.667
1936	10	1	1	.909
1937	7	4	0	.636
1938	8	3	0	.727
1939	9	2	0	.818
1940	6	4	1	.600
1941	10	1	0	.909
1942	8	2	1	.800
1943	7	2	1	.778
1944	8	2	0	.800
1945	6	4	0	.600
1946	6	5	0	.545
1947	6	5	1	.545
1948	3	9	0	.250
1949	2	10	0	.167
1950	3	9	0	.250
1951	3	9	0	.250
1952	6	6	0	.500
1953	2	9	1	.182
1954	4	8	0	.333
1955	6	6	0	.500
1956	4	8	0	.333
1957	3	9	0	.250
1958	1	10	1	.091
1959	7	5	0	.583
1960	8	4	0	.667
1961	11	3	0	.786
1962	13	1	0	.929
1963	11	2	1	.846
1964	8	5	1	.615
1965	10	3	1	.769
1966	12	2	0	.857
1967	9	4	1	.692
1968	6	7	1	.462
1969	8	6	0	.571
1970	6	8	0	.429
1971	4	8	2	.333
1972	10	4	0	.714
1973	5	7	2	.429
1974	6	8	0	.429
1975	4	10	0	.286
1976	5	9	0	.357
1977	4	10	0	.286
1978	8	7	1	.531
1979	5	11	0	.313
1980	5	10	1	.344
1981	8	8	0	.500

COACHES

1921-1949: Earl (Curly) Lambeau. 1950-1953: Gene Ronzani. 1954-1957: Lisle Blackbourn. 1958: Ray (Scooter) McLean. 1959-1967: Vince Lombardi. 1968-1970: Phil Bengtson. 1971-1974: Dan Devine. 1975-1981: Bart Starr.